Nationals Activity Book

By Peg Connery-Boyd

HawksNestPublishing.com

www.HawksNestPublishing.com

ISBN-10: 1-936562-12-X
ISBN-13: 978-1-936562-12-1

Illustrations by
Scott Waddell
www.ScottWaddellFinearts.com

Interior Layout by
Matt Haas
www.MattHaas.com

Coloring Page

Screech™ winds up for a pitch!

Match the Name

Match up the *Racing Presidents*™ mascot with his name.

George Washington

William Taft

Thomas Jefferson

Theodore Roosevelt

Abraham Lincoln

Solution is on page 49.

Follow the Ball #1

Circle the pitcher that threw a strike.

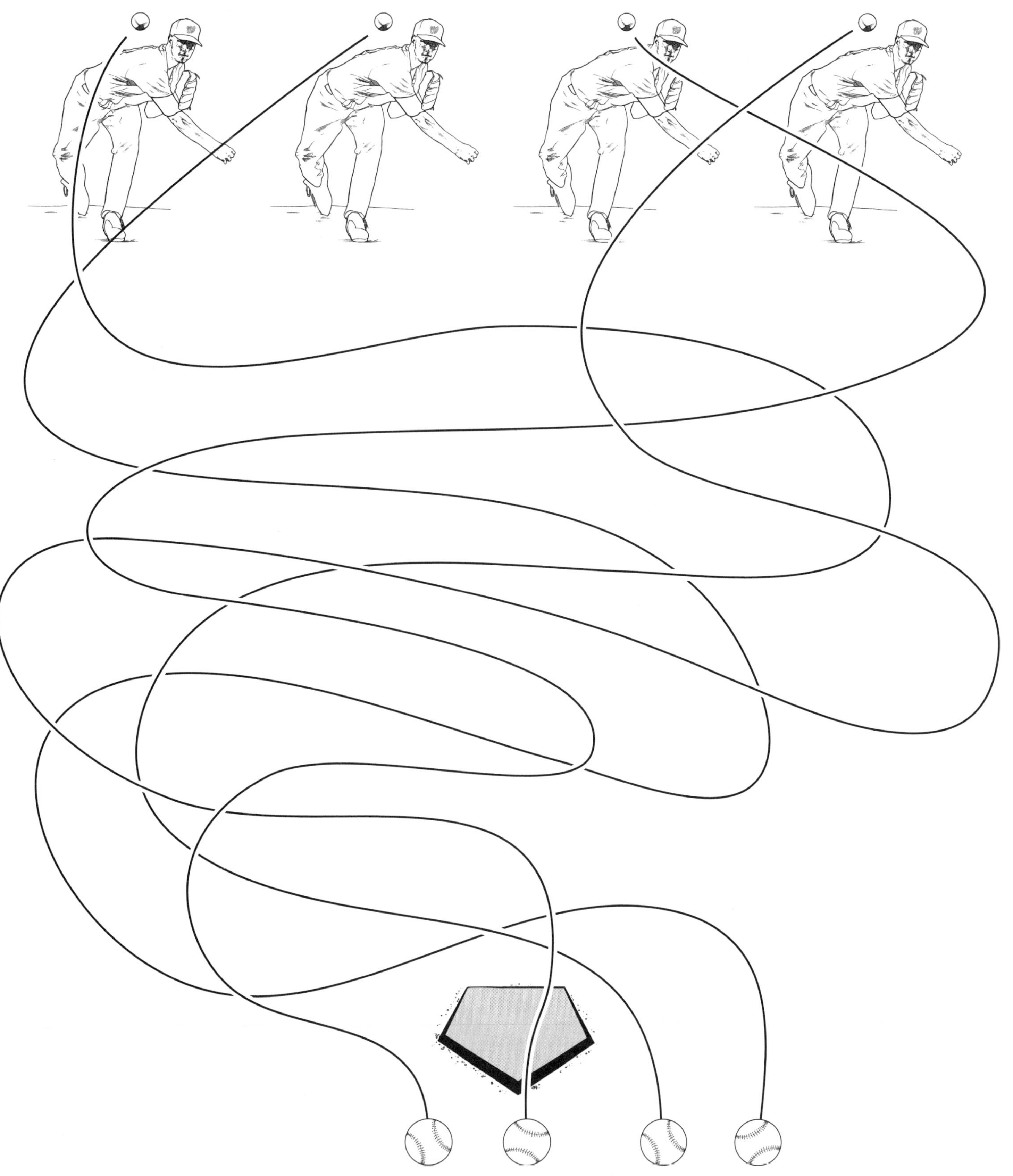

Solution is on page 49.

Connect the Dots #1

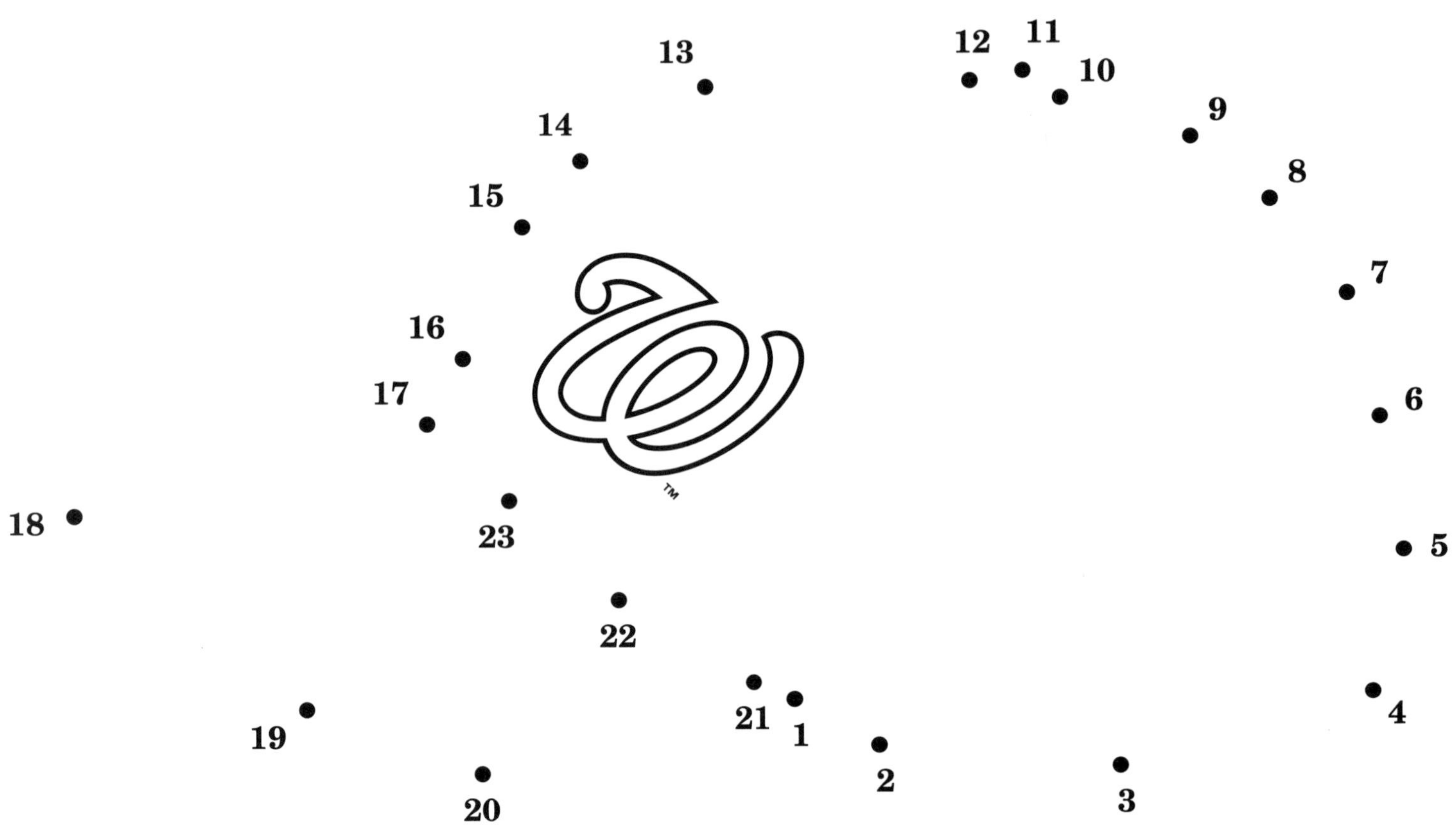

The sign of a true *Nationals* fan.

Find the Differences #1

Find three differences between the two images.

Solution is on page 50.

Maze #1

Solution is on page 50.

Find the Difference #2

Circle the image that is different.

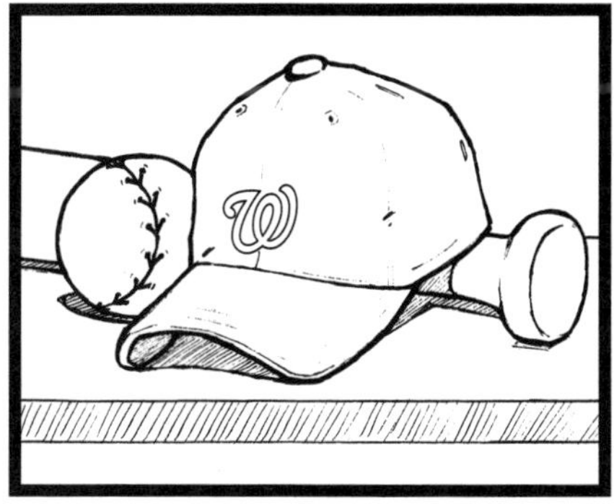
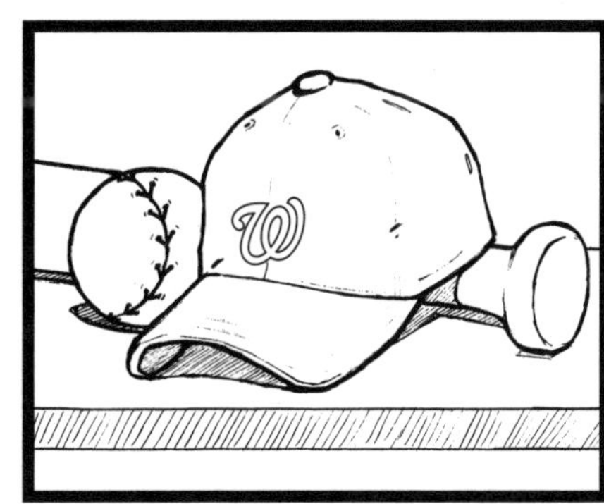
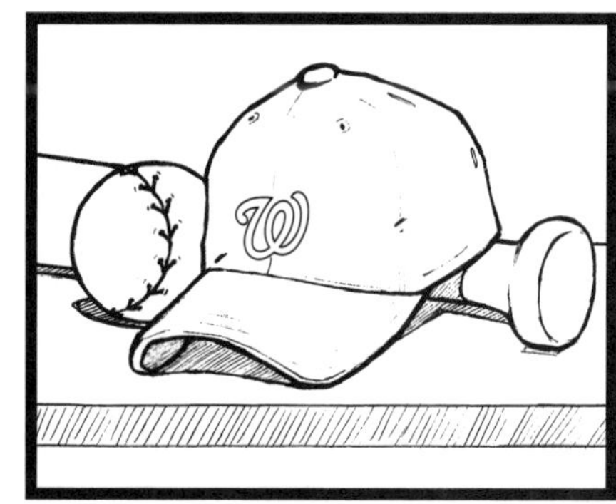

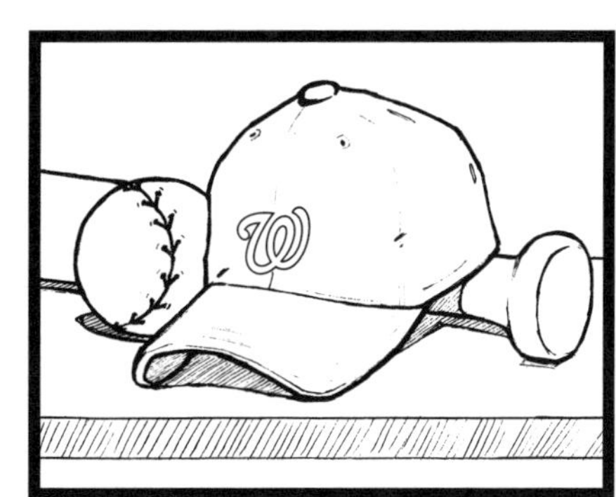
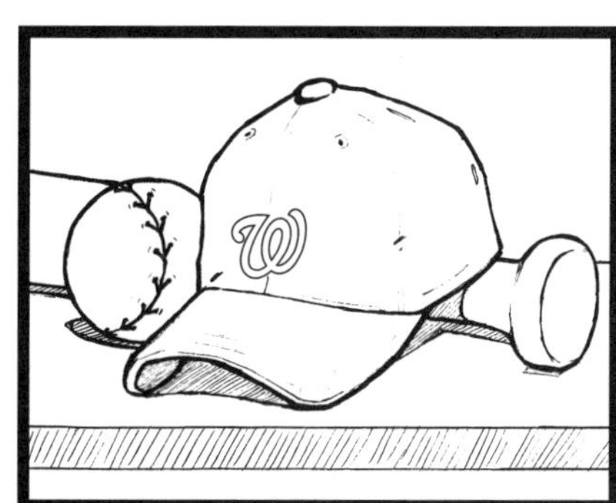
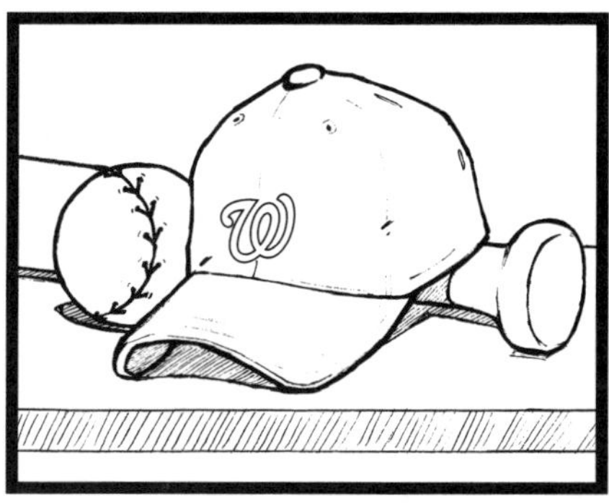
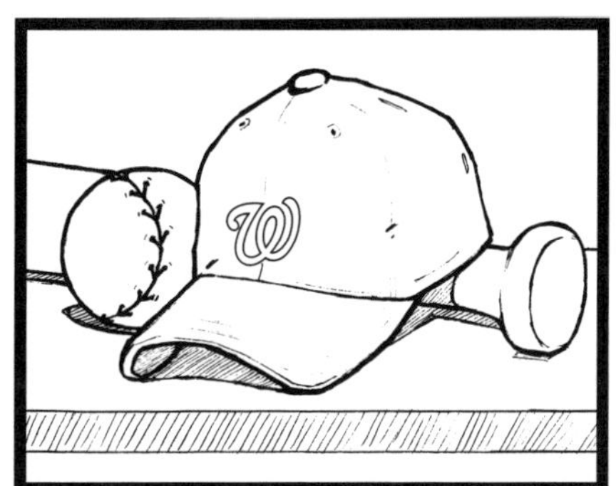

Solution is on page 51.

Draw the *Nationals* Logo

Use the grid to help you draw the *Nationals* logo!

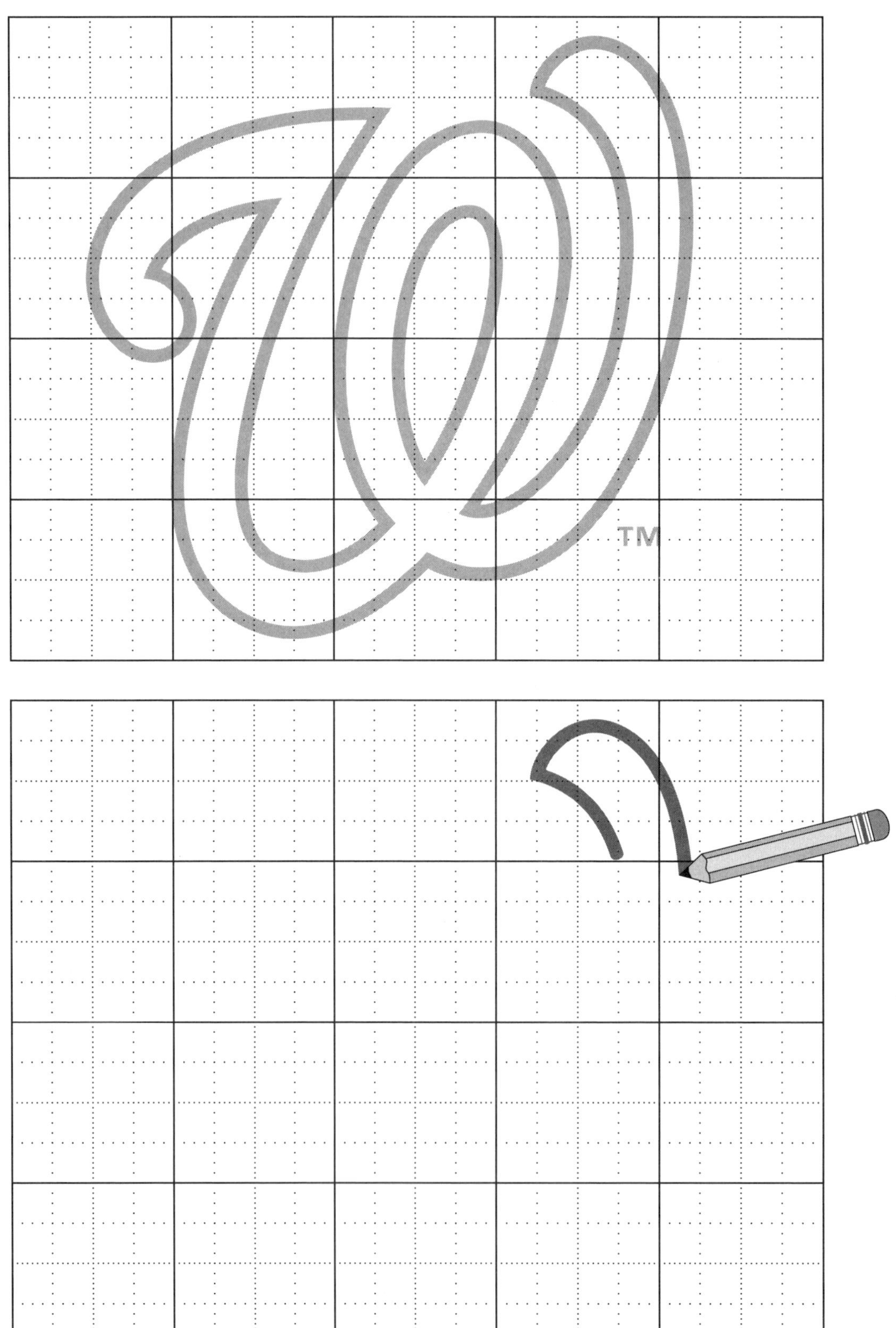

Secret Message #1

Use the key to unscramble this message.

KEY

= A	= G	= O	= U
= D	= I	= R	= Y
= E	= N	= T	

Solution is on page 51.

Label the Parts of a Baseball Field

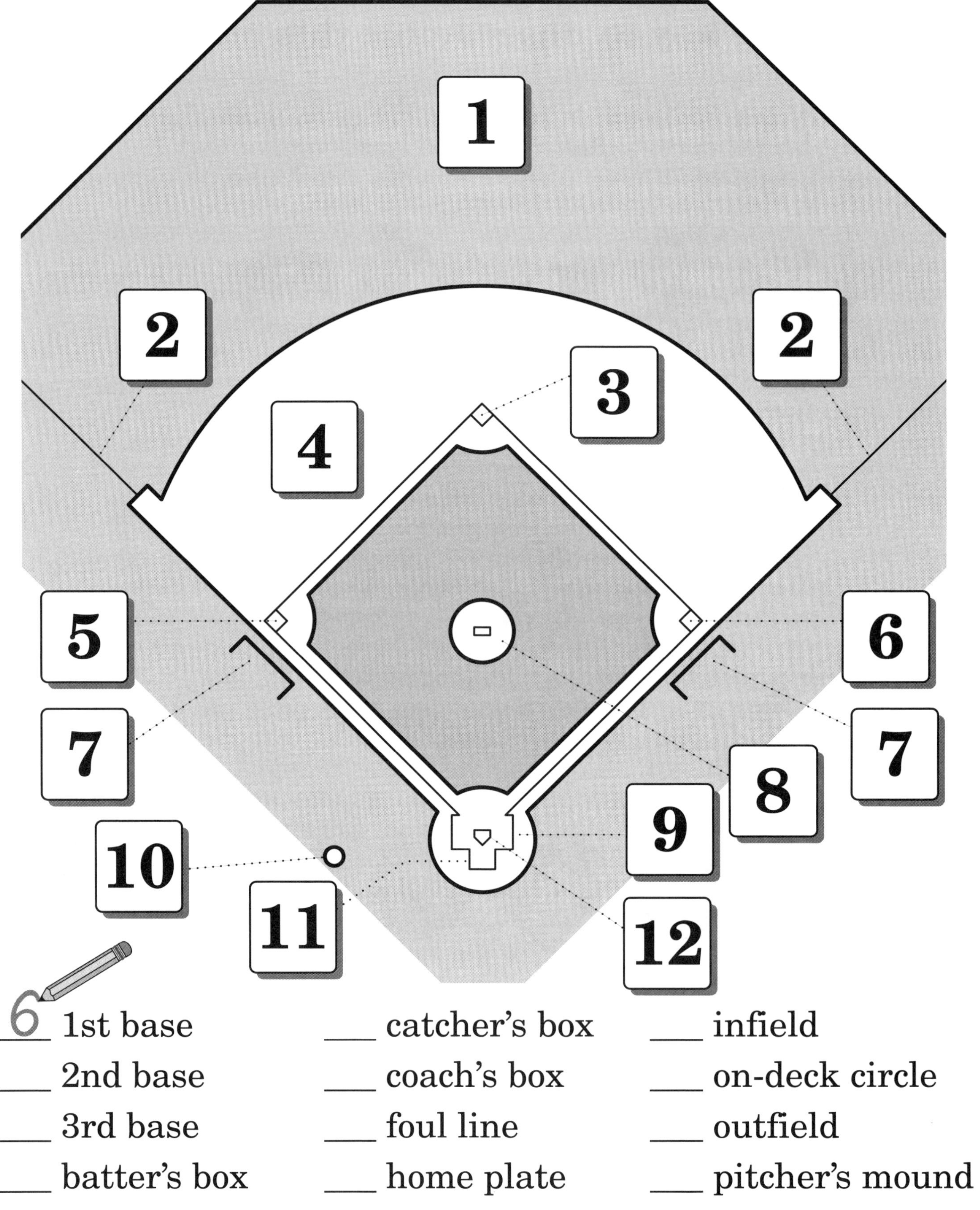

_6_ 1st base
___ 2nd base
___ 3rd base
___ batter's box

___ catcher's box
___ coach's box
___ foul line
___ home plate

___ infield
___ on-deck circle
___ outfield
___ pitcher's mound

Solution is on page 52.

Coloring Page

Nationals™ Scoreboard

Stadium Snacks Scramble

Unscramble the letters to reveal the names of these tasty stadium snacks.

DOAS

_ _ _ _

OTH GDO

_ _ _   _ _ _

ROCPOPN

_ _ _ _ _ _ _

ZEPRTEL

_ _ _ _ _ _ _

CIE MCEAR

_ _ _   _ _ _ _ _ _

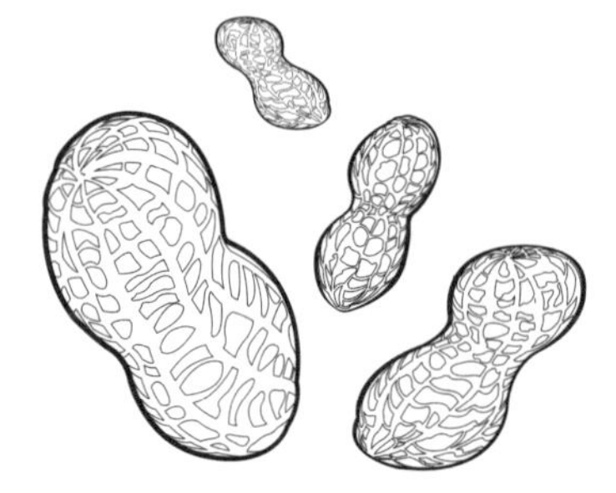

NUPTEAS

_ _ _ _ _ _ _

Solution is on page 52.

Connect the Dots #2

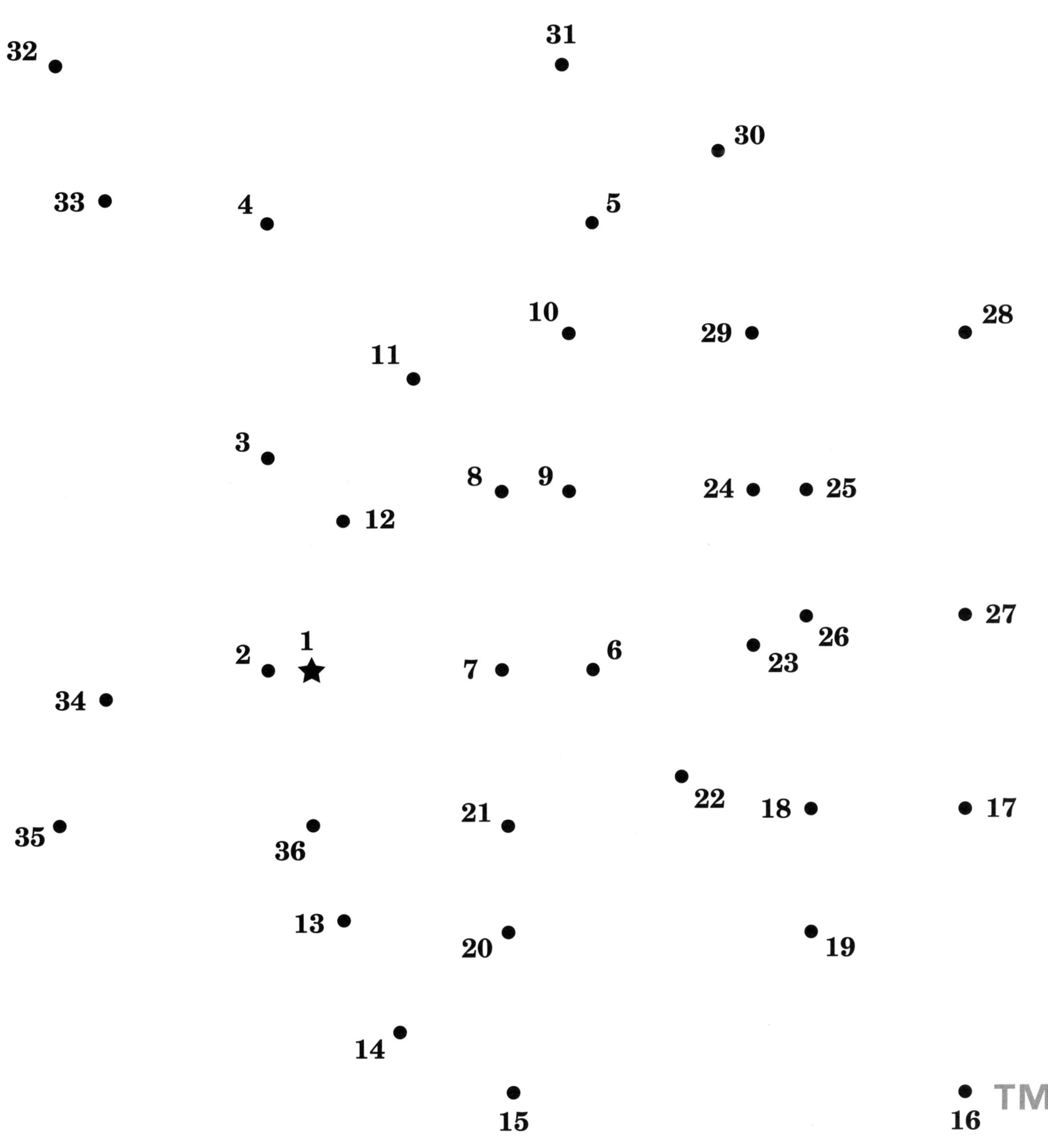

Color the *Nationals* logo!

Coloring Page

Screech™ keeps his eye on the ball!

Word Search #1

P	A	N	A	C	O	S	T	I	A	W
C	R	K	A	L	Q	N	D	Q	N	A
L	A	E	O	V	E	H	H	T	A	S
Q	T	Z	S	M	Y	C	P	D	T	H
X	Q	C	U	I	E	Y	G	N	I	I
N	W	N	E	E	D	Z	A	X	T	N
G	O	G	R	Q	Z	E	D	R	U	G
M	T	C	H	E	Q	L	N	I	D	T
F	S	T	N	W	E	E	K	T	E	O
P	A	R	K	C	R	V	X	W	S	N
D	I	S	T	R	I	C	T	D	P	L

Try to find all the words contained in the list below:

ANACOSTIA	NATITUDE	PRESIDENTS
DISTRICT	NAVY YARD	SCREECH
MONUMENT	PARK	WASHINGTON

Solution is on page 53.

Coloring Page

Batter up!

Crossword Puzzle #1 – Baseball Facts

Use your knowledge about baseball facts to solve the crossword puzzle.

Across

1. The pitcher stands on the pitcher's ________ when he throws the baseball.
5. After the batter hits the ball, he runs toward ________ base.
6. The player who throws the ball toward home plate for the batter to hit is called the ________.
9. To score a run, the player must touch ________ plate.

Down

2. The ________ calls the balls and strikes.
3. Each baseball player wears a baseball ________ on his head.
4. Three strikes and you're ________!
7. The player who crouches behind home plate is called the ________.
8. A baseball player wears a ________ on his hand to catch the ball.

Crossword Puzzle #1 – Baseball Facts

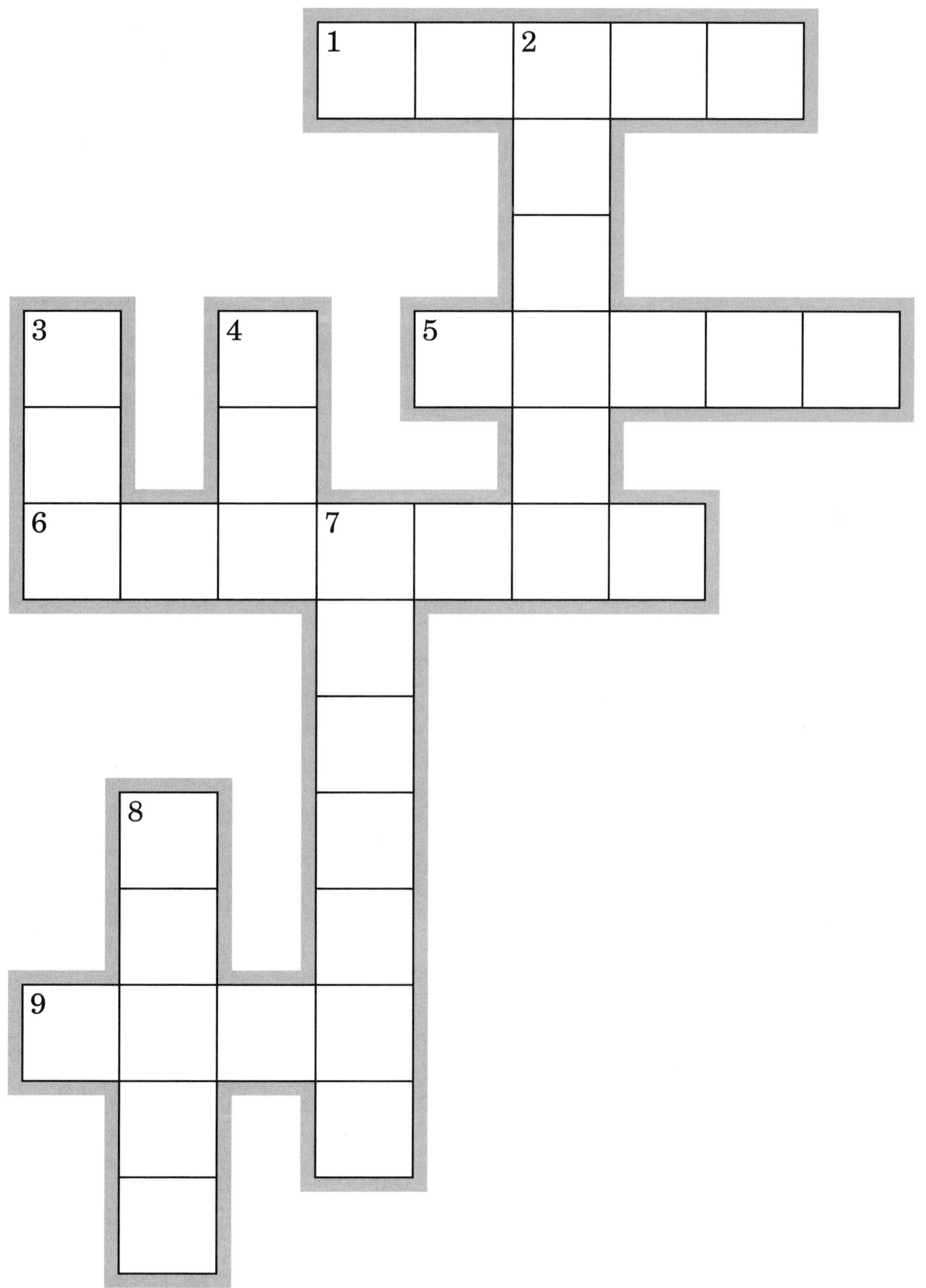

Solution is on page 53.

Connect the Dots #3

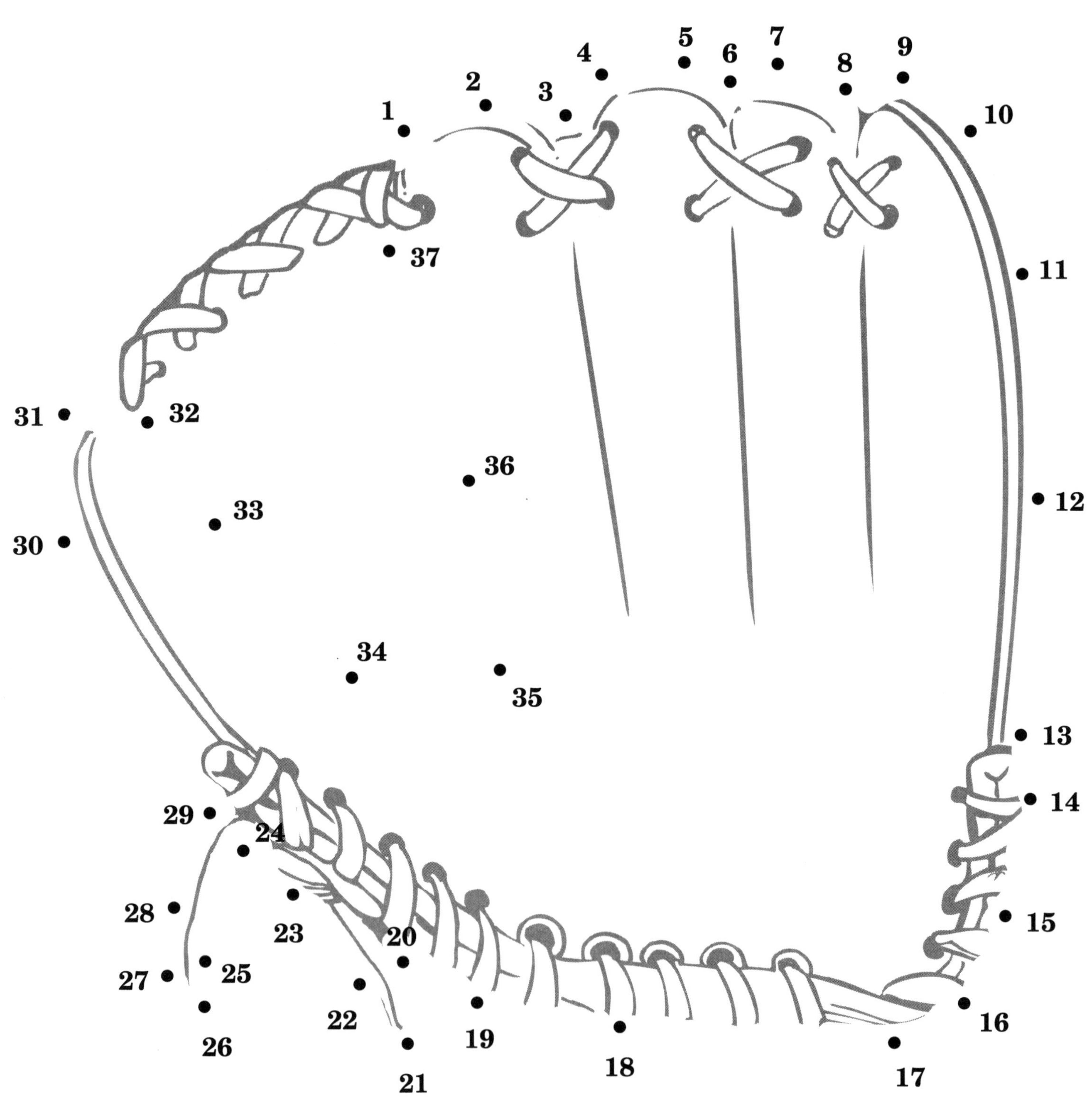

My Day at the Ballpark

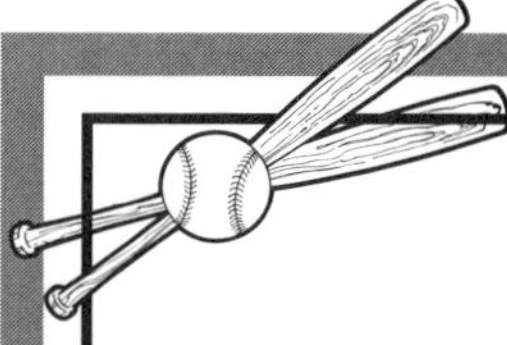

My Day at ***Nationals Park***™

By ____________________
(*your name*)

It was a ______________ day in the month of _________ .
(*weather word*) (*month*)

The *Nationals* were playing against the ______________.
(*team name*)

We took the _______ to get to Washington, D.C. for the game.
(*car / train / bus*)

I snacked on ______________ and ______________ as we watched the ballgame.
(*food*) (*food*)

I saw ________________________, my favorite player!
(*player name*)

The *Nationals* won the game! The score was ___ to ___.
(*number*)

It was a great day at *Nationals Park*™ and I can't wait to go back!

Coloring Page

Yummy Stadium Snacks

Coloring Page

A Home Run Swing!

Baseball Words Scramble

Unscramble the letters to reveal the names of these baseball words.

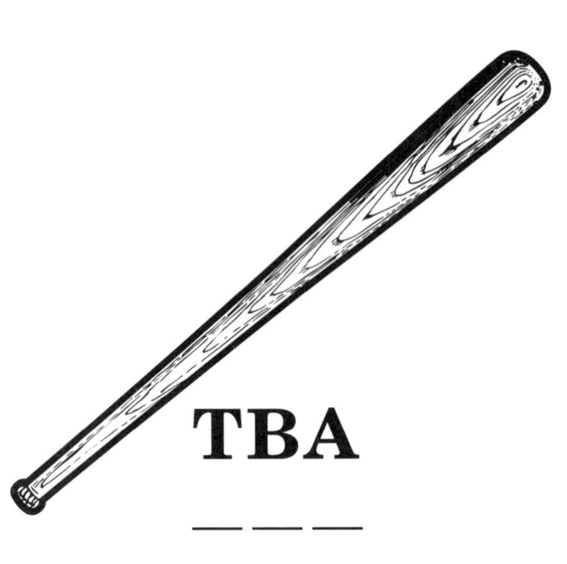

TBA

PMRIEU

APC

VOEGL

SYERJE

EBAS

Solution is on page 54.

Follow the Ball #2

Circle the batter whose ball was caught by the outfielder.

Solution is on page 54.

Secret Message #2

Use the key to unscramble this message.

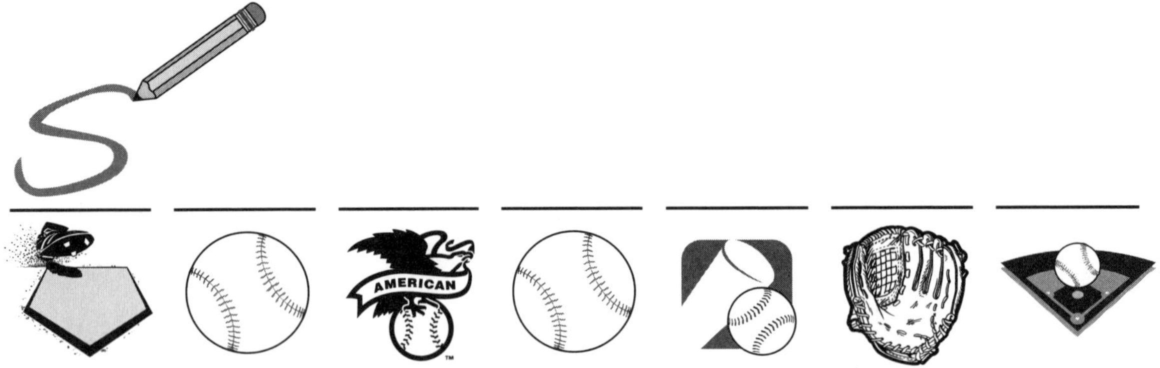

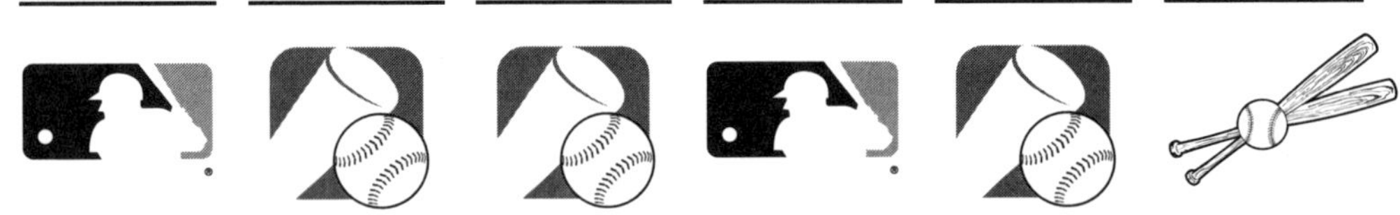

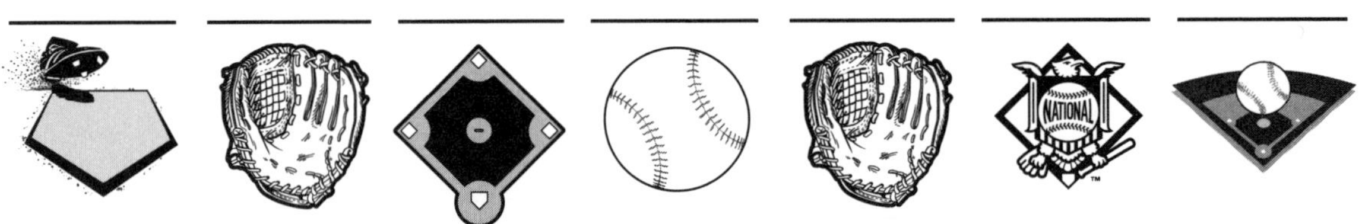

KEY

= C	= H	= R	= V
= E	= I	= S	
= G	= N	= T	

Solution is on page 55.

Word Search #2

T	T	P	L	A	Y	O	F	F	S	D
E	W	U	T	H	I	D	E	N	N	N
O	S	E	P	F	G	C	O	S	A	M
B	E	O	N	W	Y	I	R	C	S	W
F	R	L	U	A	P	A	I	M	G	G
T	I	M	D	M	T	R	U	Q	B	R
H	E	V	A	S	E	I	Y	W	F	X
D	S	H	L	M	D	B	O	L	X	T
Y	C	L	A	A	R	Z	U	N	W	U
C	A	F	T	E	Y	X	Q	Q	A	X
V	S	S	D	E	R	O	Z	O	U	L

Try to find all the words contained in the list below:

ALL STARS	DERBY	SERIES
AMERICAN	NATIONAL	STADIUMS
CHAMPIONS	PLAYOFFS	TROPHY

Solution is on page 55.

Hidden Picture #1

KEY

A = Brown B = Blue C = Purple D = Green E = Yellow F = Black

Secret Message #3

Use the key to unscramble this message.

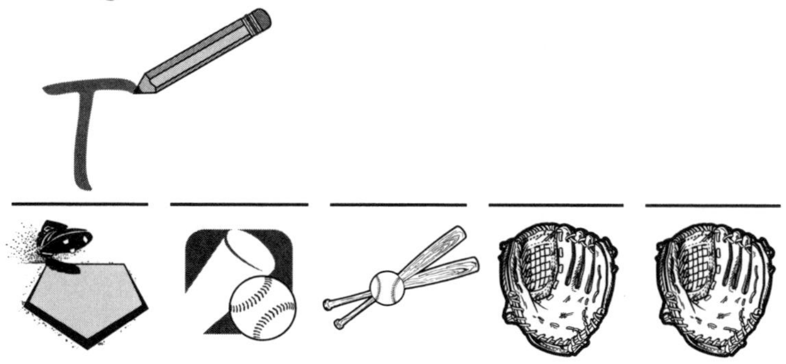

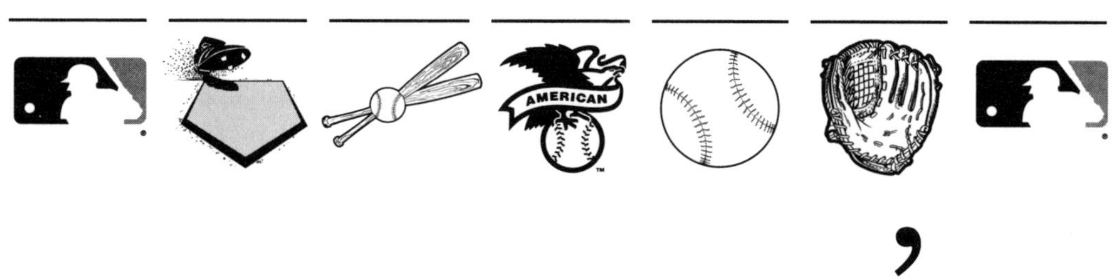

KEY

= A	= H	= N	= S	= Y
= D	= I	= O	= T	
= E	= K	= R	= U	

Solution is on page 56.

Coloring Page

Nationals Pennants

What's Inside "*Washington Nationals?*"

Make 20 new words using the letters contained in the words "*Washington Nationals.*"

W A S H I N G T O N   N A T I O N A L S

Example: HALO

Example: LOGO

1.
2.
3.
4.
5.
6.
7.
8.
9.
10.
11.
12.
13.
14.
15.
16.
17.
18.
19.
20.

Solution is on page 56.

My Page About Me

My name is ____________________.

My age is ____.

My favorite team is ____________________.

My favorite player is ____________________.

My favorite position to play is ______________.

I bat (righty / lefty).

I throw (righty / lefty).

My favorite number is ____.

Coloring Page

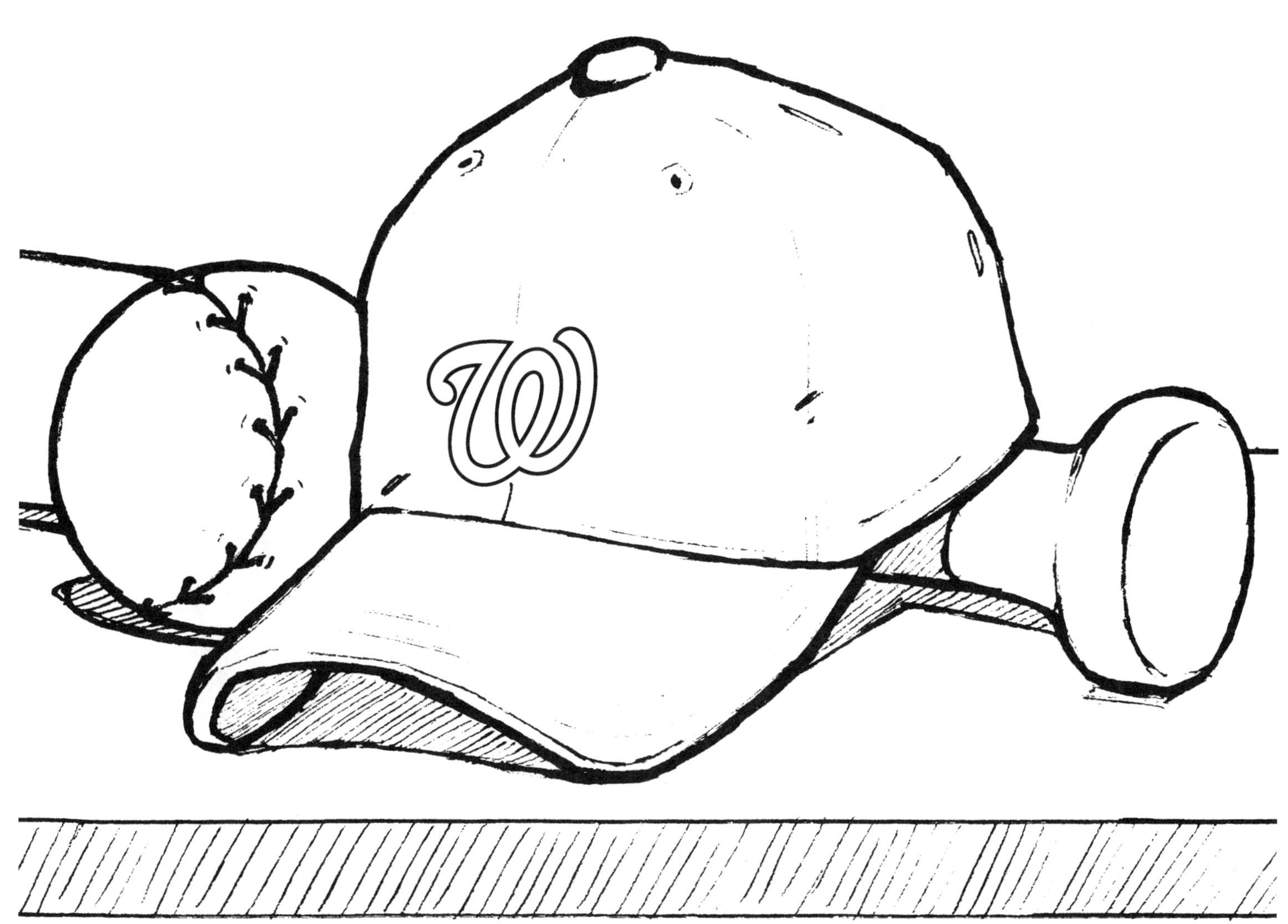

Baseball Gear

What's the Score?

Add the runs to see who wins.

Example:

	1	2	3	4	5	6	7	8	9	R
PHILLIES	0	1	0	0	2	0	0	0	0	3
NATIONALS	0	0	1	0	0	1	0	0	2	4

Game: 1

	1	2	3	4	5	6	7	8	9	R
PHILLIES	0	0	0	0	1	0	2	0	0	
NATIONALS	0	2	0	0	1	0	1	1	0	

Game: 2

	1	2	3	4	5	6	7	8	9	R
PHILLIES	0	0	1	0	0	0	0	1	0	
NATIONALS	0	3	0	0	2	0	0	0	2	

Game: 3

	1	2	3	4	5	6	7	8	9	R
PHILLIES	0	3	1	2	0	1	0	1	0	
NATIONALS	0	1	0	1	2	0	1	0	1	

Game: 4

	1	2	3	4	5	6	7	8	9	R
PHILLIES	1	1	1	0	1	0	3	0	0	
NATIONALS	0	4	1	0	1	1	0	0	2	

Solution is on page 57.

Maze #2

Solution is on page 57.

Draw the *MLB* Logo

Use the grid to help you draw the *MLB* logo!

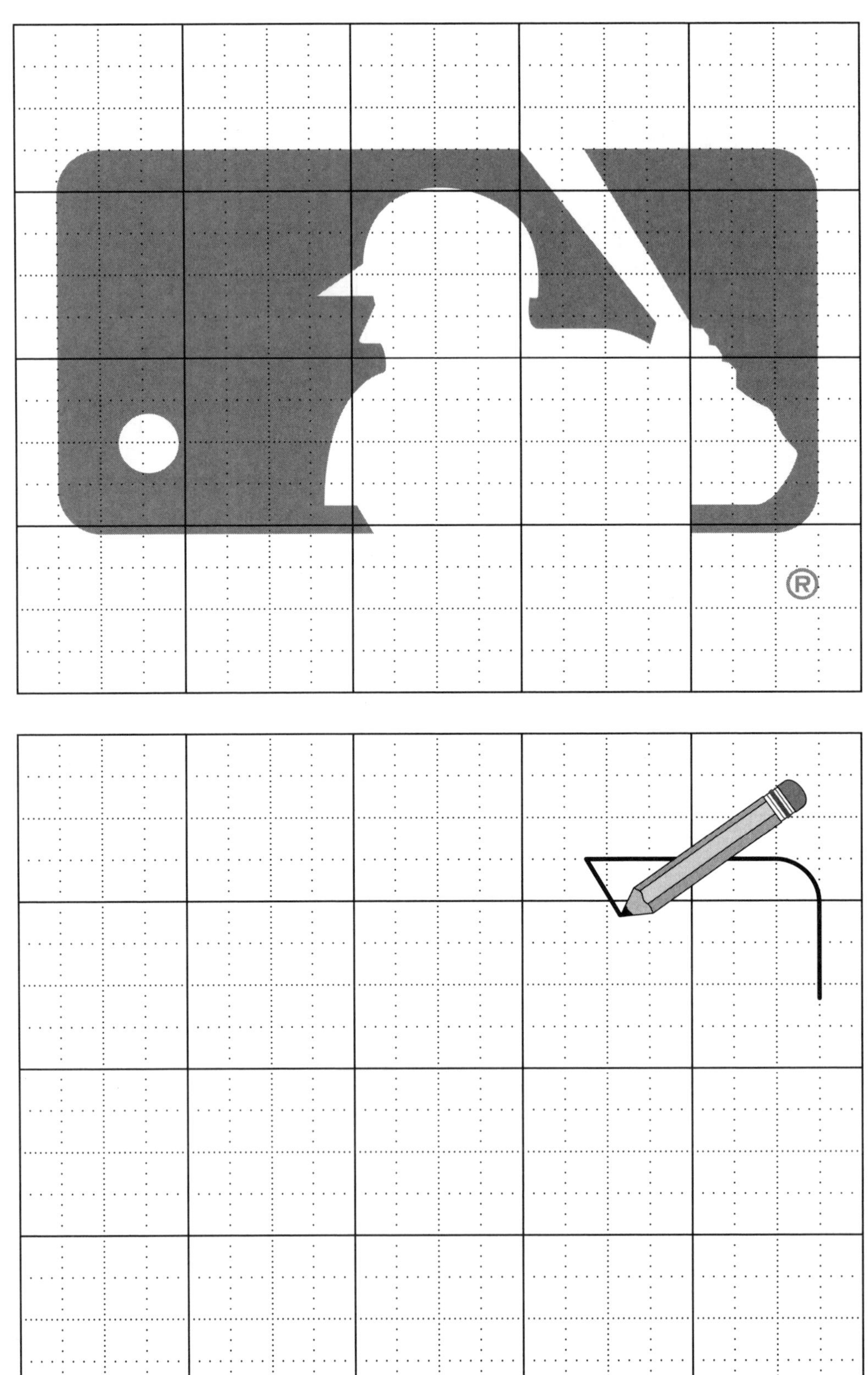

Word Search #3

D	S	V	U	G	E	D	Y	O	R	C
O	C	Z	Y	T	I	S	Z	C	A	R
G	O	U	A	W	T	B	E	Q	N	I
Y	R	T	E	M	H	P	N	L	G	V
L	E	A	G	L	E	I	O	V	C	E
E	B	W	Q	S	Q	T	T	G	D	R
J	O	L	T	N	I	U	N	E	E	F
S	A	A	U	P	D	I	K	O	Q	R
P	R	W	A	E	C	A	M	X	Q	O
V	D	C	R	A	W	C	I	J	R	N
C	B	S	R	W	K	N	A	T	S	T

Try to find all the words contained in the list below:

BLUE	NATS	RIVERFRONT
CAPITOL	RACING	SCOREBOARD
EAGLE	RED	WHITE

Solution is on page 58.

Coloring Page

One Lucky *Nationals* Fan!

Secret Message #4

Use the key to unscramble this message.

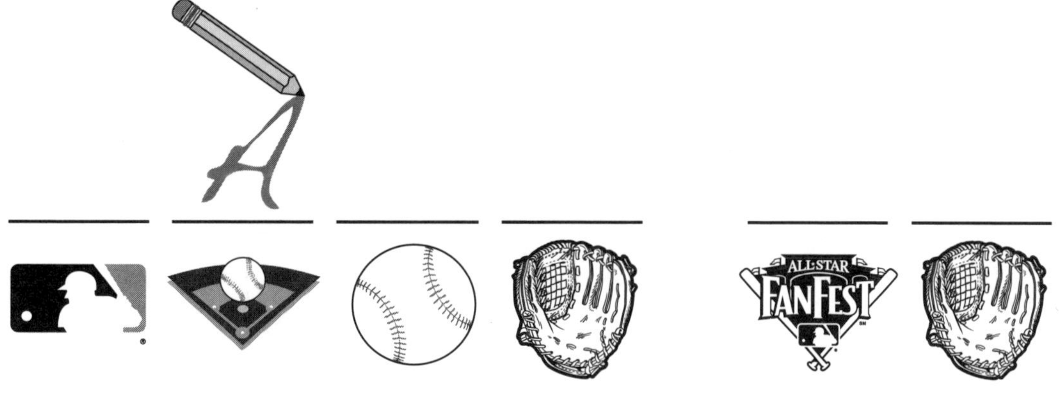

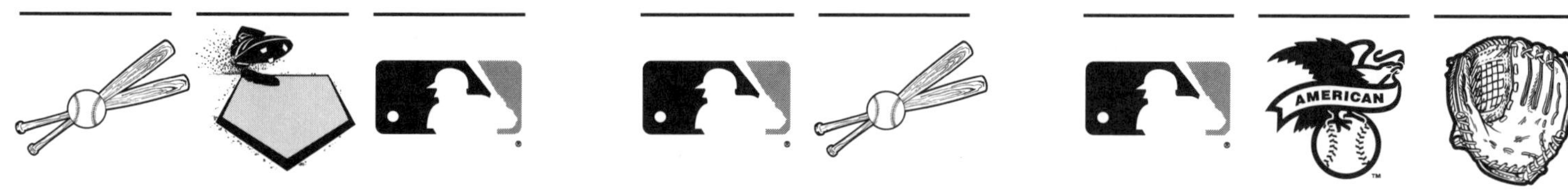

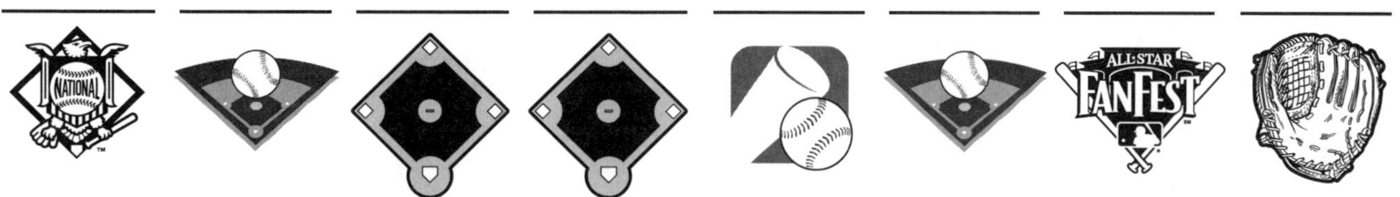

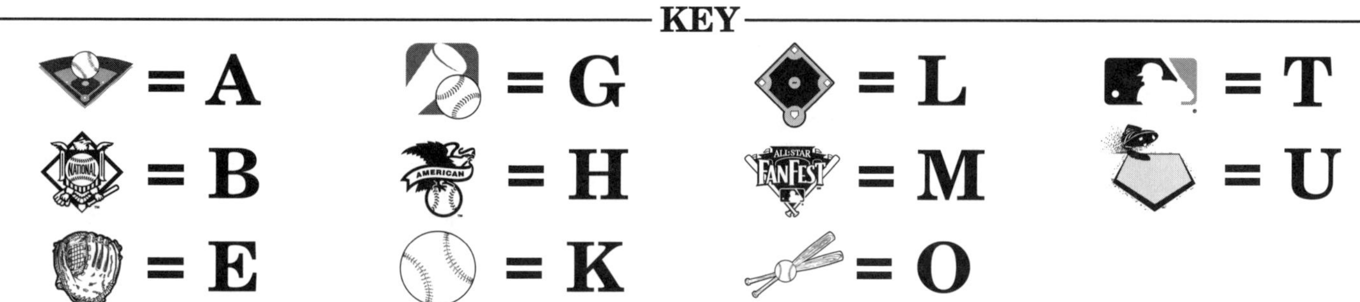

Solution is on page 58.

Find the Differences #3

Find four differences between the two images.

Solution is on page 59.

Baseball Positions Scramble

Unscramble the letters to reveal the names of these baseball positions.

ITCHREP

PITCHER

RIFTS

SABMANE

CAHTERC

ERTTAB

TUOLIEFDRE

Solution is on page 59.

What's Inside "*Major League Baseball?*"

Make 20 new words using the letters contained in the words "*Major League Baseball.*"

M A J O R L E A G U E B A S E B A L L

Example: AREA

Example: BEAR

1 ____

2 ____

3 ____

4 ____

5 ____

6 ____

7 ____

8 ____

9 ____

10 ____

11 ____

12 ____

13 ____

14 ____

15 ____

16 ____

17 ____

18 ____

19 ____

20 ____

Solution is on page 60.

Maze #3

Follow the maze to the correct exit to find out if the batter is out or safe.

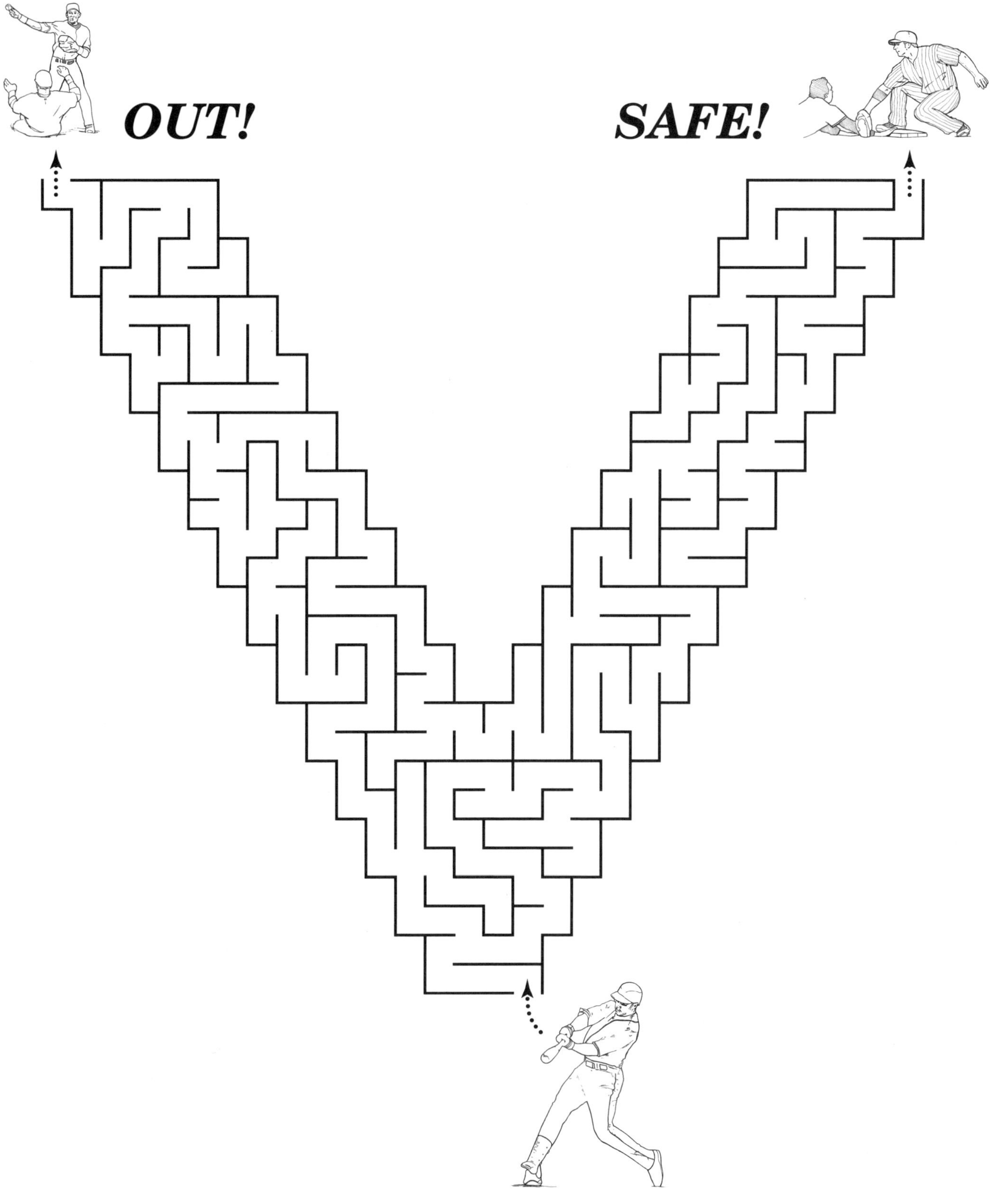

Solution is on page 60.

Crossword Puzzle #2 – *Nationals* Facts

Use your knowledge about the *Nationals* Facts to solve the crossword puzzle.

Across

1. You can see the Washington _________ from the upper decks of *Nationals Park*.
3. A frequently used nickname for the *Nationals* is the _________.
5. The macot of the *Nationals* is an _________, which is also the national bird of the United States of America.
6. The local rivals of the *Washington Nationals* are the _________, only 45 miles away.
8. The *Nationals* play in the *National League* _________ *Division*.

Down

2. One popular slogan for *Nationals* fans at the ballpark is “Ignite your _________!”
4. *Nationals Park* is located near the _________ River.
7. The name of the *Nationals* mascot is _________.

Crossword Puzzle #2 – *Nationals* Facts

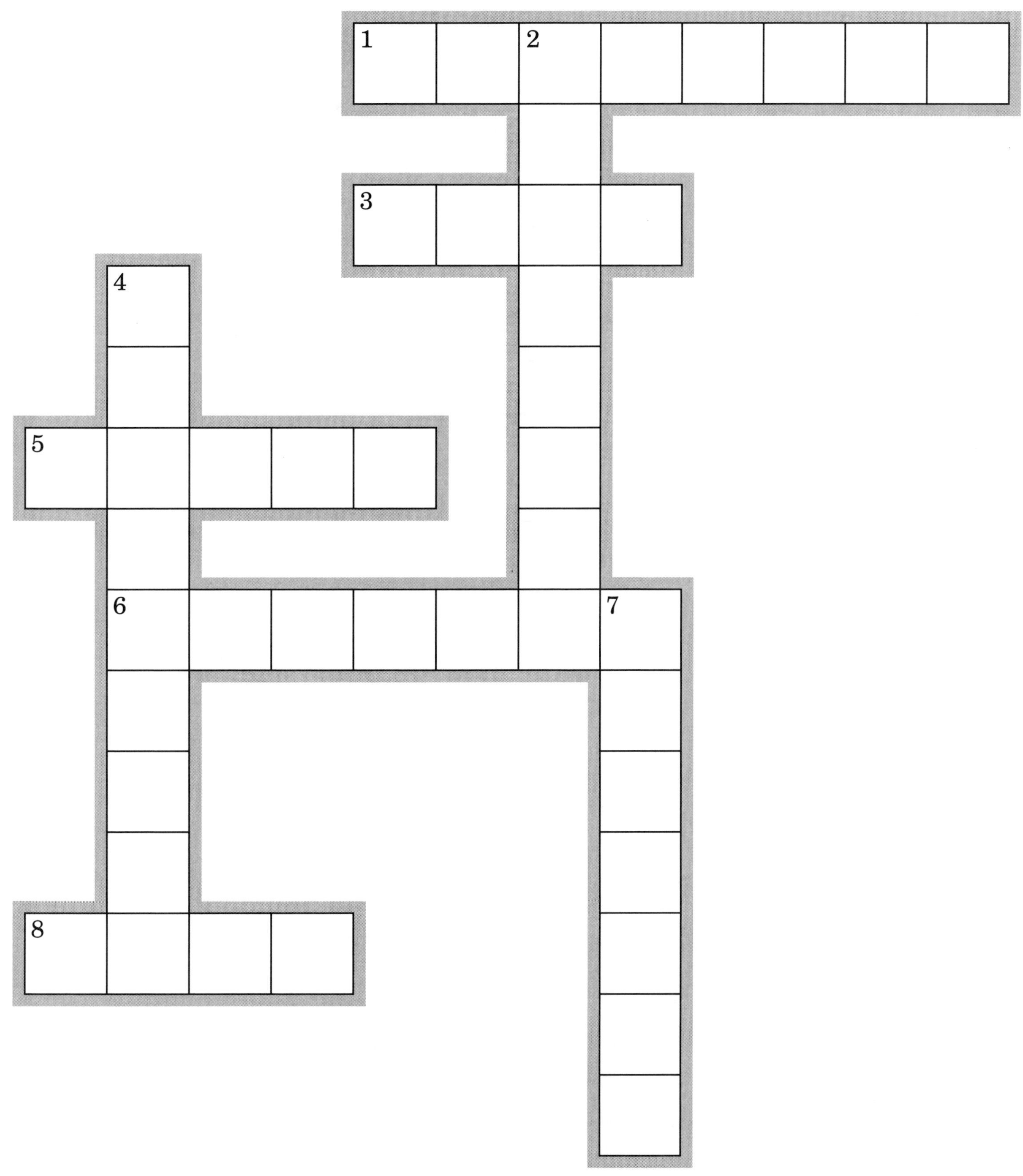

Solution is on page 61.

Hidden Picture #2

KEY

A = Dark Blue B = Light Blue C = Light Grey D = Dark Grey (or black) E = Tan

Word Search #4

C	T	J	I	Q	U	E	K	R	R	W
P	A	I	U	D	L	Z	K	T	L	V
E	M	T	G	P	U	H	C	U	P	B
N	Z	S	C	M	B	G	O	A	T	A
U	P	Y	T	H	L	F	O	K	P	S
C	C	D	U	R	E	Y	B	U	I	E
F	V	W	U	R	I	R	S	I	T	B
O	W	K	I	O	V	K	E	R	C	A
Q	X	P	G	L	O	V	E	Q	H	L
E	M	Z	D	R	G	Z	X	T	E	L
U	Z	S	O	G	S	M	T	N	R	Q

Try to find all the words contained in the list below:

BASEBALL	DUGOUT	PITCHER
CAP	FOUL	STRIKE
CATCHER	GLOVE	UMPIRE

Solution is on page 61.

Find the Difference #4

Circle the image that is different.

Solution is on page 62.

Solutions to Puzzles

Solution to Match the Name Game, page 2

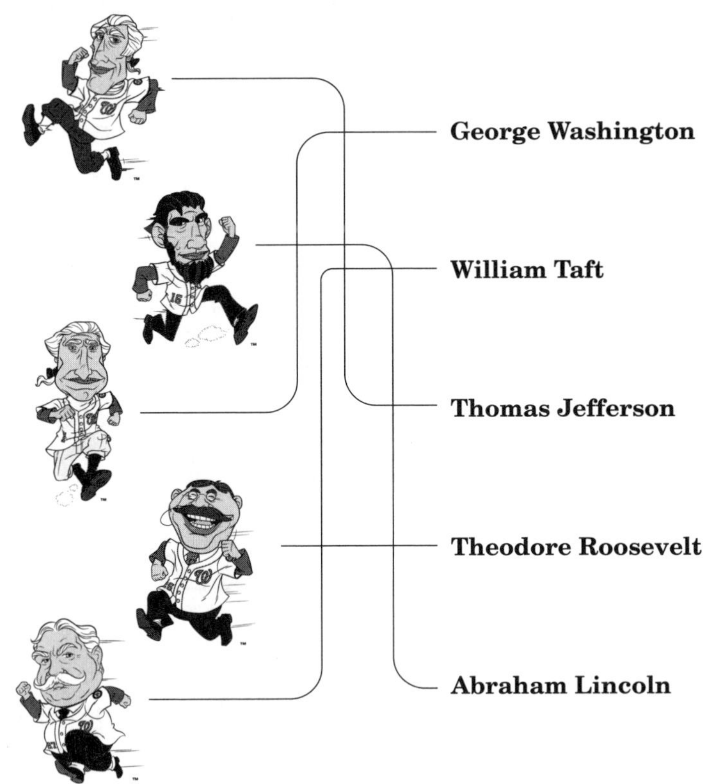

Solution to Follow the Ball #1, page 3

Solution to Find the Differences #1, page 5

Solution to Maze #1, page 6

Solution to Find the Difference #2, page 7

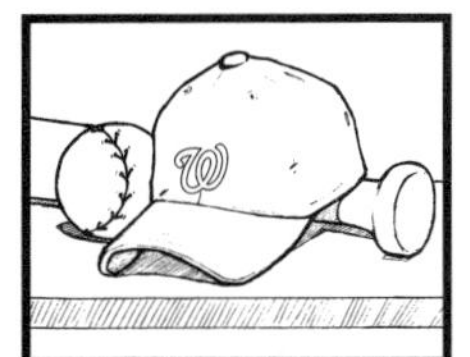
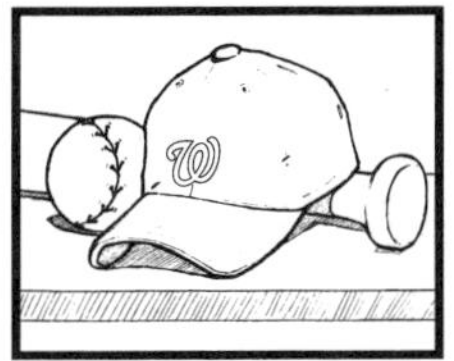

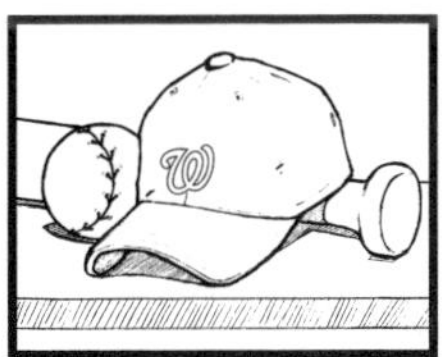
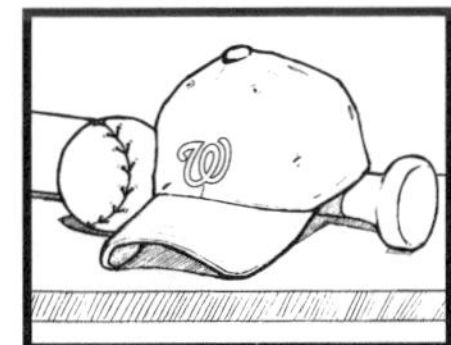
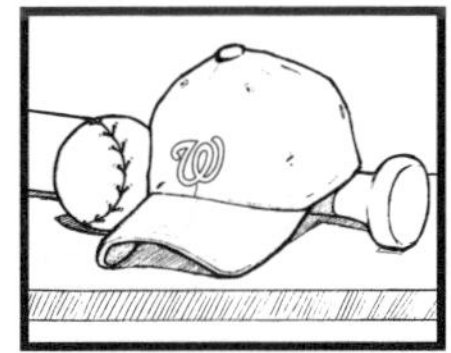

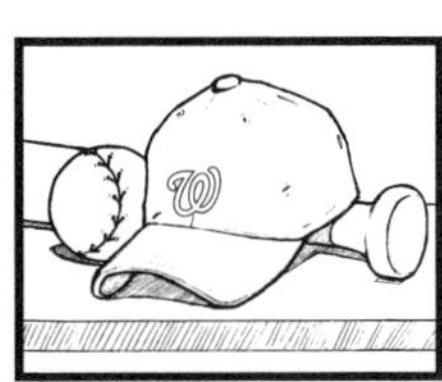
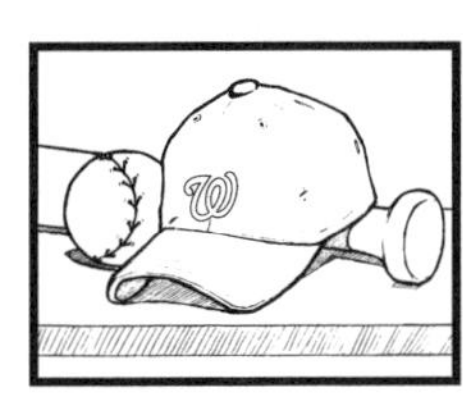
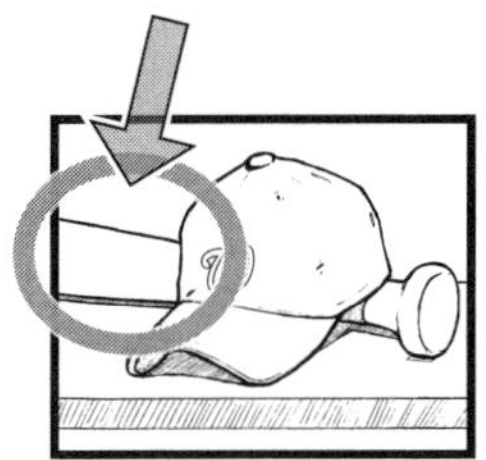

Solution to Secret Message #1, page 9

KEY

= A	= G	= O	= U
= D	= I	= R	= Y
= E	= N	= T	

Solution to Label the Parts of a Baseball Field, page 10

6	1st base	11	catcher's box	4	infield
3	2nd base	7	coach's box	10	on-deck circle
5	3rd base	2	foul line	1	outfield
9	batter's box	12	home plate	8	pitcher's mound

Solution to Stadium Snacks Scramble, page 12

Solution to Word Search #1, page 16

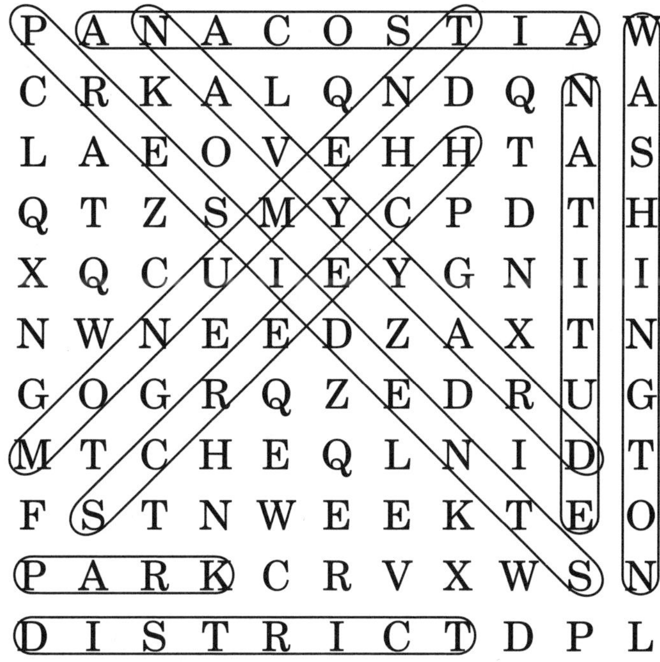

Try to find all the words contained in the list below:

ANACOSTIA	NATITUDE	PRESIDENTS
DISTRICT	NAVY YARD	SCREECH
MONUMENT	PARK	WASHINGTON

Solution to Crossword Puzzle #1 - Baseball Facts, page 19

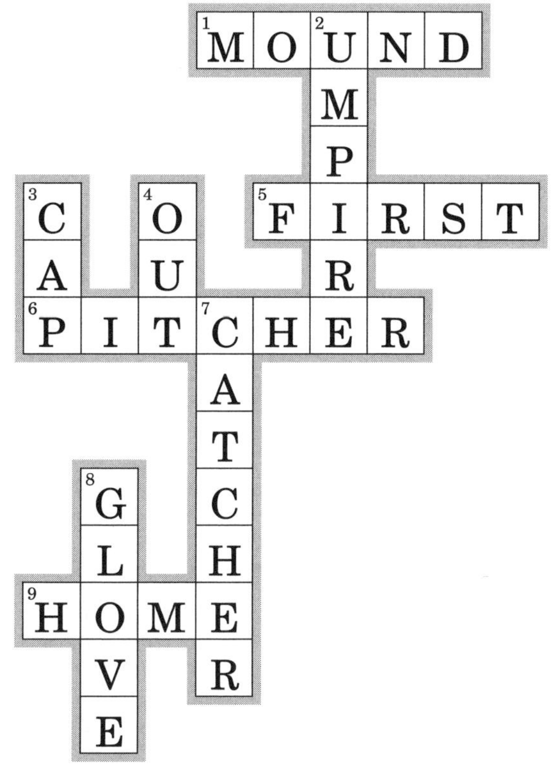

Solutions to Baseball Words Scramble, page 24

Solution to Follow the Ball #2, page 25

Solution to Secret Message #2, page 26

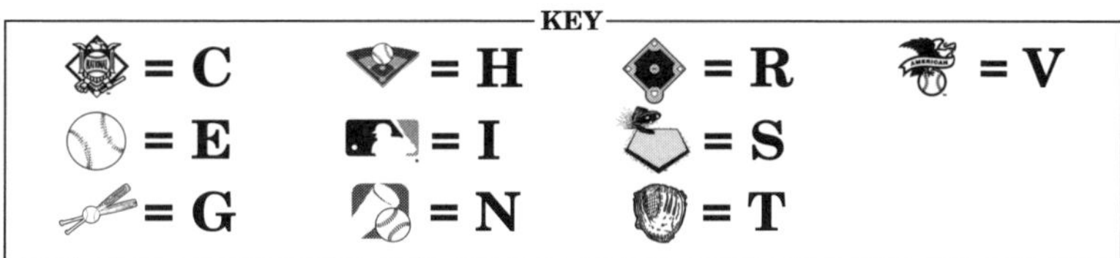

Solution Word Search #2, page 27

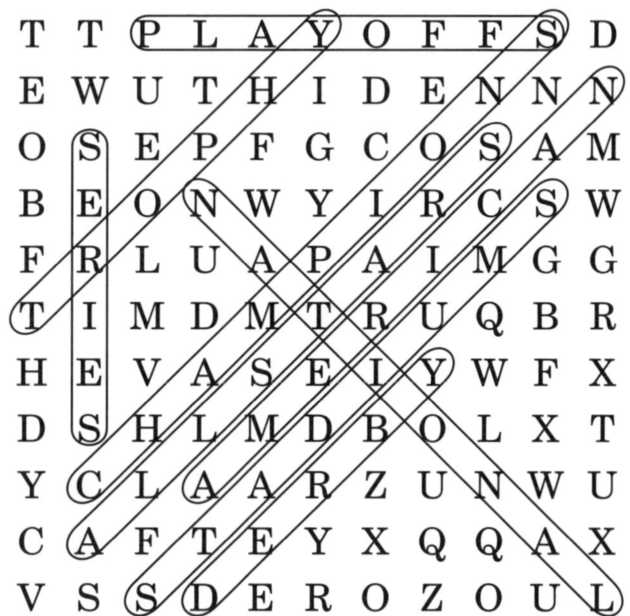

Try to find all the words contained in the list below:

ALL STARS	DERBY	SERIES
AMERICAN	NATIONAL	STADIUMS
CHAMPIONS	PLAYOFFS	TROPHY

Solution to Secret Message #3, page 29

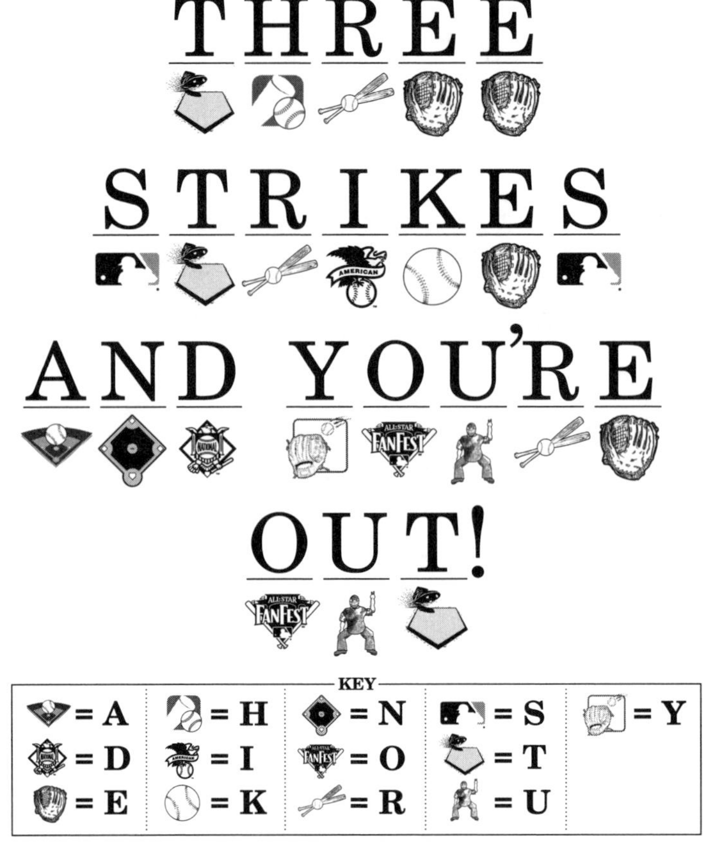

Solution to What's Inside *Washington Nationals*, page 31

Below are just a few examples of words that could be made with these letters.

W A S H I N G T O N   N A T I O N A L S

also	hang	loan	shin	snow	that	wait
gain	hiss	long	show	soil	thin	want
glow	into	loot	sign	solo	this	wash
goal	lash	nail	silo	song	tilt	what
goat	last	onto	sing	soon	tint	wilt
gown	lawn	saga	slit	swan	tool	wing
hail	lint	sail	slot	swig	toss	wish
halo	lion	salt	slow	tail	town	with
halt	list	sang	snag	than	twig	wool

Solution to What's the Score?, page 34

Game: 1

	1	2	3	4	5	6	7	8	9	R
PHILLIES	0	0	0	0	1	0	2	0	0	3
NATIONALS	0	2	0	0	1	0	1	1	0	5

Game: 2

	1	2	3	4	5	6	7	8	9	R
PHILLIES	0	0	1	0	0	0	0	1	0	2
NATIONALS	0	3	0	0	2	0	0	0	2	7

Game: 3

	1	2	3	4	5	6	7	8	9	R
PHILLIES	0	3	1	2	0	1	0	1	0	8
NATIONALS	0	1	0	1	2	0	1	0	1	6

Game: 4

	1	2	3	4	5	6	7	8	9	R
PHILLIES	1	1	1	0	1	0	3	0	0	7
NATIONALS	0	4	1	0	1	1	0	0	2	9

Solution to Maze #2, page 35

Solution to Word Search #3, page 37

```
D S V U G E D Y O R C
O C Z Y T I S Z C A R
G O U A W T B E Q N I
Y R T E M H P N L G V
L E A G L E I O V C E
E B W Q S Q T T G D R
J O L T N I U N E E F
S A A U P D I K O Q R
P R W A E C A M X Q O
V D C R A W C I J R N
C B S R W K N A T S T
```

Try to find all the words contained in the list below:

BLUE	NATS	RIVERFRONT
CAPITOL	RACING	SCOREBOARD
EAGLE	RED	WHITE

Solution to Secret Message #4, page 39

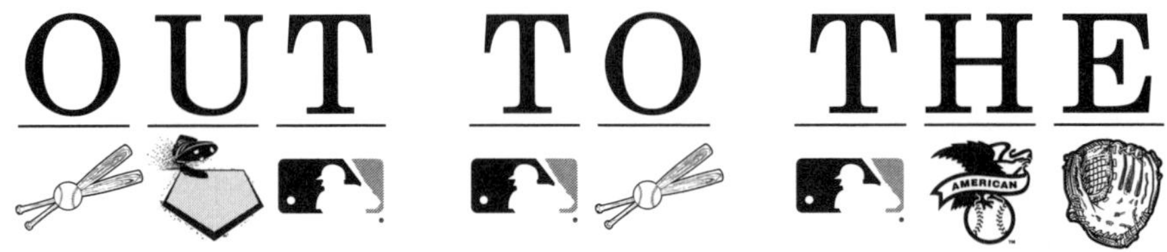

KEY

= A	= G	= L	= T
= B	= H	= M	= U
= E	= K	= O	

Solution to Find the Differences #3, page 40

Solution to Baseball Positions Scramble, page 41

Solution to What's Inside *Major League Baseball*, page 42

M A J O R   L E A G U E   B A S E B A L L

ajar	beam	bull	gore	meal	reel	seem
alas	bear	ease	lamb	mole	roll	sell
also	bell	else	lame	mule	rule	slab
area	blob	game	lobe	muse	saga	slam
aura	blue	gear	lube	ogre	sage	soar
ball	blur	germ	lure	oral	sale	some
barb	boar	glee	male	rage	seal	sour
bare	bomb	glue	mall	real	seam	urge
base	bulb	goal	mars	ream	sear	user

Solution to Maze #3, page 43

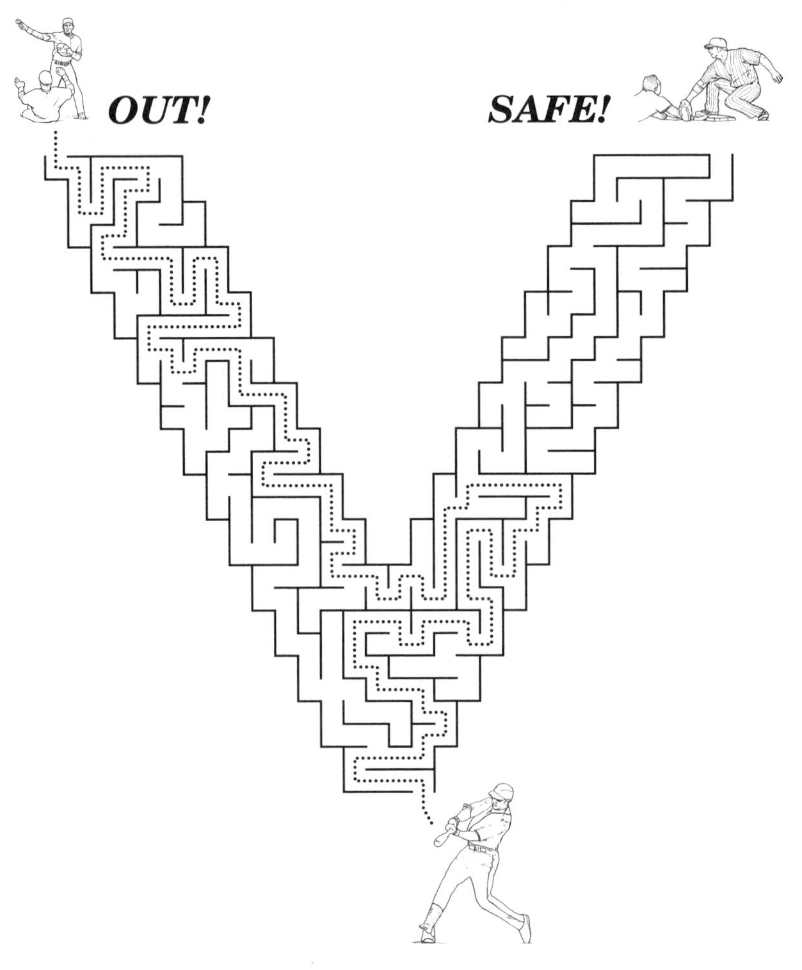

Solution to Crossword #2 - *Nationals* Facts, page 45

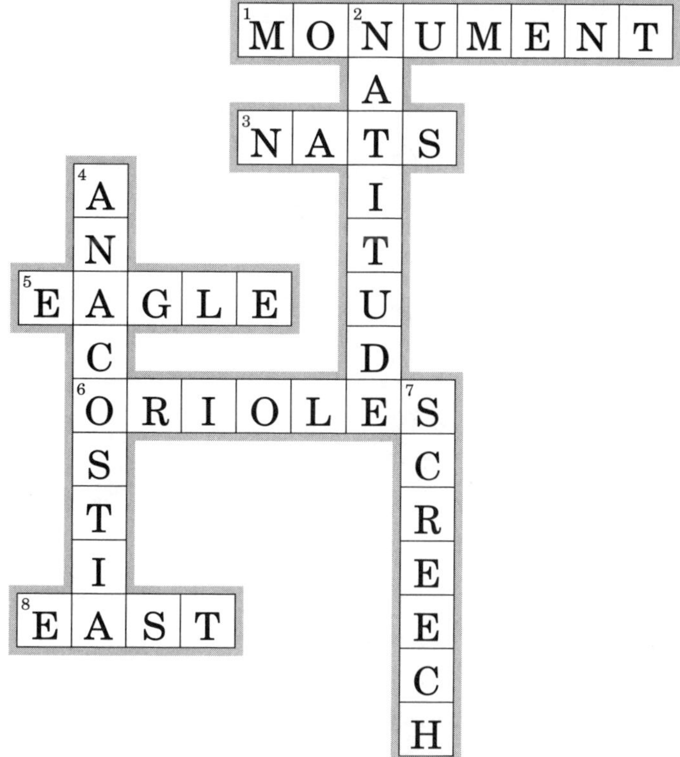

Solution to Word Search #4, page 47

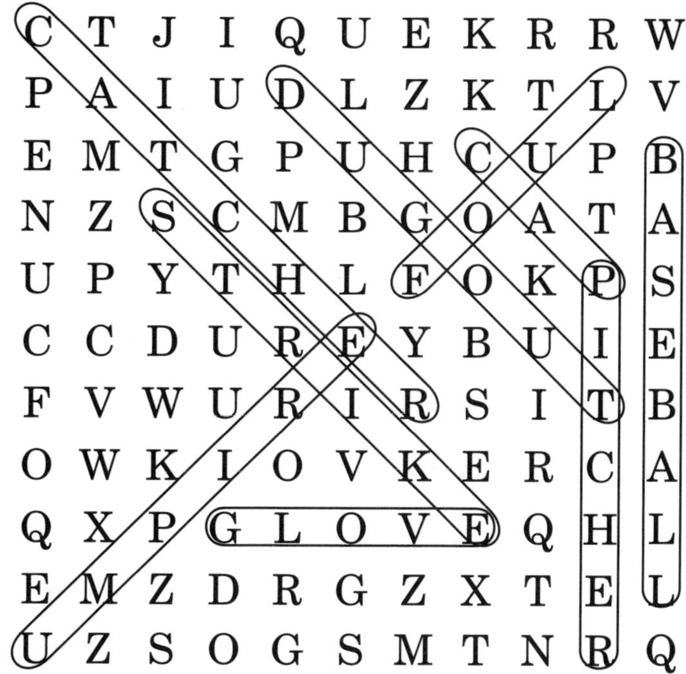

Try to find all the words contained in the list below:

BASEBALL	DUGOUT	PITCHER
CAP	FOUL	STRIKE
CATCHER	GLOVE	UMPIRE

Solution to Find the Difference #4, page 48

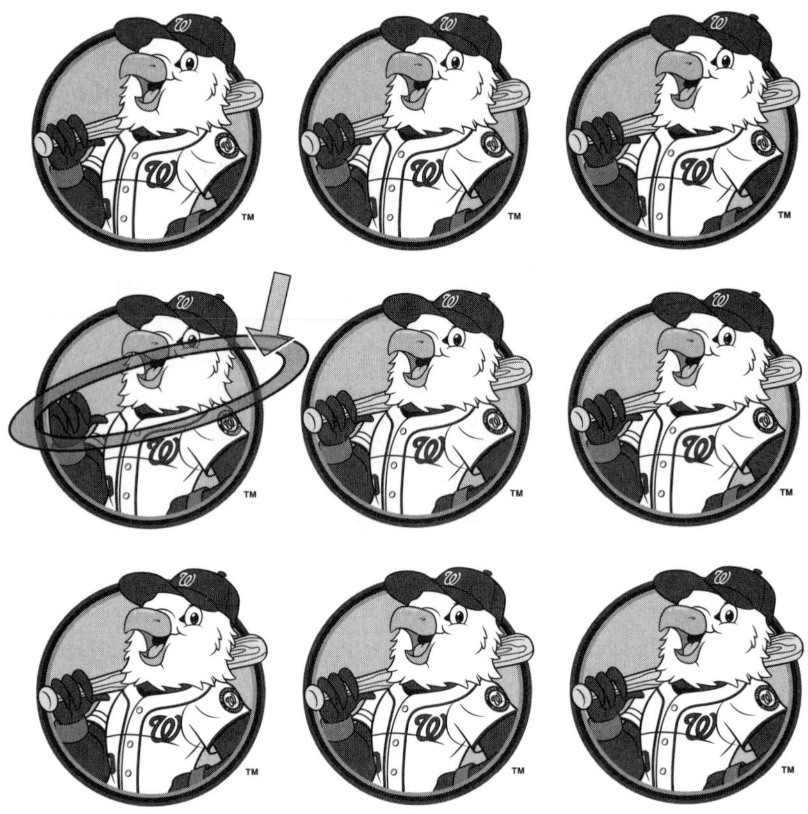

We hope that you enjoyed the
Washington Nationals
Activity Book!

Please contact us with questions or comments:

Hawk's Nest Publishing LLC
85 B Wall Street
Madison, CT 06443
www.HawksNestPublishing.com
facebook.com/HawksNestPub
Twitter: @HawksNestPub

Books for the Young and Young at Heart...